Paleo Salad Dressing for Novice Chefs: 25 Delicious Recipes That Are Healthy and Ready in a Flash

Disclaimer and Terms of Use: Effort has been made to ensure that the information in this book is accurate and complete, however, the author and the publisher do not warrant the accuracy of the information, text and graphics contained within the book due to the rapidly changing nature of science, research, known and unknown facts and internet. The Author and the publisher do not hold any responsibility for errors, omissions or contrary interpretation of the subject matter herein. This book is presented solely for motivational and informational purposes only.

Table of Contents

Mayo Recipes

Ingredients:

- 4 egg yolks
- 3 T cider vinegar
- 1 tsp salt
- 1 tsp ground mustard
- 3 C avocado oil
- 1 ½ T lemon juice

Directions:

I.   Whisk the egg yolks until well beaten
II.   Add the vinegar and whisk a little bit more
III.   Add remaining ingredients and whisk
IV.   Add to air tight container and store in fridge

Lemon Vignette

Ingredients:

- 1/3 C olive oil
- Lemon juice
- 2 tsp raw honey
- 1 tsp Dijon mustard
- 1 T minced garlic

Directions:

I. Whisk together the ingredients in a bowl and store in fridge

Asian Dressing

Ingredients:

- ½ C cold water
- ¼ C fish sauce
- ¼ C rice vinegar
- 2 T lime juice
- 2 ½ T coconut sugar
- 2 T minced garlic
- 1 tsp serrano Chile

Directions:

I. Combine your ingredients in a jar and mix or shake
II. Store in cold area

Fig Vinaigrette

Ingredients:

- ¼ C dried figs
- ½ C balsamic vinegar
- 1 T Dijon mustard
- ¼ C olive oil
- Salt and pepper to taste

Directions:

I. Blend everything in a food processor or blender, blend until smooth
II. Season with salt and pepper to taste

Mock Ranch dressing

Ingredients:

- ½ C soaked, and drained cashers
- 1 C coconut milk
- ½ tsp garlic powder
- ½ tsp onion powder
- ½ tsp salt and pepper to taste
- 1 T chopped chives
- ½ tsp dill weed

Directions:

I. Blend your cashews in food processor or blender until they are like paste like
II. Ad coconut milk and continue to blend, and the rest of the ingredients and keep blending until completely smooth
III. Serve cold

Olive and Chive Dressing

Ingredients:

- 1 T hemp oil
- 1 T chopped chives
- 1 T EVOO
- 1 tsp red wine vinegar
- 1 T minced garlic
- ½ tsp honey

Directions:

I. Whisk everything together and store in cool area, serve over great salads

Tarragon Dressing

Ingredients:

- ¼ C tarragon
- 2 shallots
- 4 T minced garlic
- 1 C EVOO
- ½ C champagne vinegar
- 2 T lemon juice
- 1 tsp Dijon mustard
- ½ tsp salt and pepper

Directions:

I.   Add everything to a bowl and whisk for several minutes, add seasonings and continue to whisk

Fennels

Ingredients:

- 1 bowl arugula
- ½ C blackberries
- Fennels stemmed and chopped

Dressing

- 1 T olive oil
- 1 T organic Dijon mustard
- 2 tsp raw syrup
- Pepper to taste

Directions:

I. Add your salad mix first into a bowl,
II. Toss your dressing ingredients together and drizzle over fennel salad

Pink Vinaigrette

Ingredients:

- 1 ½ C EVOO
- ¼ C red balsamic vinegar
- ¼ C white balsamic vinegar
- 2 tsp Dijon mustard
- 2 T minced garlic
- 1 tsp salt and pepper to taste

Directions:

I. Add everything together, but your garlic and whisk well,
II. Stir in your garlic last
III. Keep cold and serve with salad

Rosemary Dressing

Ingredients:

- 1 pint chopped strawberries
- 1 T EVOO
- ½ lemon juice
- 1 tsp minced rosemary
- ¼ tsp salt and pepper
- 1 tsp poppy seeds
- 5 C arugula leaves, chopped

Directions:

I.   Add everything but the arugula into your blender and chop

II. Blend until everything is smooth stir in poppy seeds which is optional

III. Serve with the arugula or house salad

Dijon Vinaigrette

Ingredients:

- 1 T apple cider vinegar
- 2 T olive oil
- 1 tsp. Dijon mustard
- ½ tsp ground ginger
- ½ tsp ground parsley
- Salt and pepper to taste

Directions:

I.   Add everything together and blend until smooth,
II.   Pour into glass jar and shake
III.   Store in cold area

Paleo Caesar Salad

Ingredients:

- 2 egg yolks
- 2 T lemon juice
- 1 T minced garlic
- 2 tsp yellow mustard
- ¼ tsp mustard
- ¼ tsp horseradish
- 2 tsp anchovy paste
- ½ tsp dried parsley
- Salt and pepper to taste
- 3 T EVOO

Directions:

I.   Blend everything but the EVOO in your food processor or blender
II.   Slowly add in EVOO
III. Store in fridge, good for no more than 3 days max.

Tex Mex Dressing

Ingredients:

- 1 tsp taco seasoning
- 2 tsp coconut milk
- 3 T crushed tomato

Directions:

I.   Blend everything together, or whisk together.
II.   Serve and store in cold area

Herb Dressing

Ingredients:

- 1 C soaked macadamias
- ¾ C coconut water
- 1/3 C lemon juice
- 2 T minced garlic
- 1 tsp onion powder
- 1 tsp dried parsley
- 1 tsp dried dill
- 1 T chopped chives
- ½ tsp salt and pepper to taste

Directions:

I.   Real simple, add everything in to your blender, blend until really creamy and smooth,

II.   Serve cold over your favorite salad

Orange Carotene Dressing

Ingredients:

- ½ lbs. carrots, chopped
- ¼ C fresh ginger
- 2 T chopped onion
- ¼ C seasoned rice vinegar
- 1 T soy sauce
- 1 T sesame oil
- ½ tsp. salt and pepper to taste
- 12 C coconut oil

Directions:

I.   Add everything into your blender or food processor and blend until smooth, almost creamy

Greens Salad

Ingredients:

- 1 T olive oil
- 1 tsp balsamic vinegar
- ½ tangerine juiced
- ½ lime, juiced

Directions:

I. Whisk everything together and serve cool, toss with your salad

Avocado Dressing

Ingredients:

- 1 Avocado
- 3 T minced garlic
- 1 can coconut milk
- 1 T lemon juice
- ¼ tsp salt and pepper to taste
- 2 T fresh dill
- 2 T fresh chives
- ¼ tsp paprika
- ¼ tsp cayenne pepper

Directions:

I. Blend your peeled avocado until chopped
II. Add everything else in to your blend and blend pulse
III. Store pureed dressing into refrigerator

Vinaigrette

Ingredients:

- ¾ C balsamic vinegar
- 1 T minced garlic
- 1 tsp dried oregano
- 2 tsp Dijon mustard
- ¾ C EVOO
- Salt and pepper to taste

Directions:

I. Add everything in to a mason jar and tighten lid, and shake well
II. Store in cold fridge

Tomato Vinaigrette

Ingredients:

- 1 C lemon vinaigrette (recipe below)
- 1 pint cherry tomatoes
- 1 T minced garlic

Directions:

I.   Add everything into your blender or food processor and blend until creamy

Lemon Vinaigrette

Ingredients:

- 3 T lemon juice
- ½ tsp Dijon mustard
- ¾ C EVOO
- Salt and pepper to taste

Directions:

I.   Blend until smooth, and creamy store in cold area

Ground pepper Vinaigrette

Ingredients:

- ¾ C balsamic vinegar
- 1 T minced garlic
- 1 tsp dried oregano
- 2 tsp Dijon mustard
- ¾ C EVOO
- Salt and pepper to taste

Directions:

I. Blend everything together in food processor or blender until smooth

Tomato Juice Vinaigrette

Ingredients:

- 1 C lemon vinaigrette
- 1 pint cherry tomatoes
- 1 T minced garlic

Directions:

I. Add everything in to blender until smooth and serve over favorite salad

Hot Sauce for salad

Ingredients:

- 1 T minced garlic
- 1 onion, chopped
- 7 T olive oil
- ½ C diced tomatoes
- Lemon juice
- 2 tsp chopped basil

Directions:

I.   Add everything into sauce pan and cook on low heat, do not let burn, let liquids blend and thicken into a dressing

Walnut Dressing

Ingredients:

- 3 T raspberry vinegar
- ½ tsp Dijon mustard
- ¾ C walnut oil
- 2 T chopped walnuts
- Salt and pepper to taste

Directions:

I. Blend everything together in food processor blender until smooth
II. Store in cold area

Made in the USA
Las Vegas, NV
22 October 2021